Recession Proof Your Life

Six Simple Habits

By

Reynaldo J. Aguilar

© Copyright 2022 by Reynaldo Aguilar – All rights reserved.

It is not legal to reproduce, duplicate, or transmit any part of this document in either electronic means or printed format. Recording of this publication is strictly prohibited.

This book is dedicated to:

This book is dedicated to everyone who has suspended, put-off, or forfeited living their best life for far too long. No time is better than now to live the life you've hoped and dreamed about. Who would have thought it was this simple…

Table of Contents

Introduction 1

Chapter One: In Our Life Time 2

Chapter Two: Habit #1 4

Chapter Three: Habit #2 6

Chapter Four: Habit #3 8

Chapter Five: Habit #4 10

Chapter Six: Habit #5 12

Chapter Seven: Habit #6 14

Chapter Eight: Conclusion 16

Acknowledgments 17

About the Author 18

Introduction

Congratulations on having the courage to do something about the current situation. There are so many who are stuck in the rut of complaining about the current situation but take no steps to change it. Unfortunately, this is the majority of people today! I've come to realize there are two types of people in the world, those who let things happen and then there are those who make things happen! By reading this book you clearly are one to make things happen.

With all the talk about a looming recession fear and uncertainty begin to take their place at everyone's dinner table. The know-it-alls in Washington and in the media are sounding more and more like end-time prophets. They say things like 'Americans need to brace themselves' or 'these are unprecedented times,' everything short of run for the hills. What does all this mean? How is this going to affect our lives? Should I cancel my trip to Cabo next week? I've been saving for this vacation for so long!

I can succumb to the doom and gloom experts and base my life on the speculations of others or continue to Recession Proof My Life. I choose independence and the wisdom God has given me to live free, free in the ultimate sense of the word! This book is a simple approach to a very important issue we face numerous times in our lifetime. It's about living your best life and preserving the quality of life you want to live all packaged up in six simple habits!

Chapter One: In Our Life Time

Another Recession

Here we go again another economic downturn. Just when I felt like things were getting back to normal. I should have known something was wrong when gas prices hit six bucks. And then everything that is going on in the ports, you don't need to be an economic expert to know this is not looking good!

There's a lot of debate right now about us entering a recession. Some say we've already been in a recession for some time. Others are saying it's just begun. They do agree that a recession is on the horizon. That word carries so much weight that it instantly strikes panic in people. People's first reaction to hearing about entering a recession is to think about the security of their jobs, people get frugal in their spending. It's almost like a natural reflex when people hear the word recession.

Why people react so negatively is because of the impact recessions of the past have had on people's lives. Whether you understand the factors that contributed to a recession or not doesn't matter you still feel the effects of it in your personal life. Recessions of the past have been responsible for job losses, extended periods of unemployment, lower household incomes, reduced wages & benefits, and even ending relationships in divorce. These aren't minor issues; these are major life changing events. Since so much could be at stake it's only right we try and understand what a recession is.

We don't need to be an economist to have a working knowledge of what a recession is. A simple Google search will explain recession as:

"A period of ***temporary*** economic decline during which trade and industrial activity are reduced, generally identified by a fall in GDP in two successive quarters."

I bolded and italicized the word temporary to highlight the fact that a recession has always been temporary. According to the National Bureau of Economic Research, an agency that keeps track of this stuff says the average U.S. recession has lasted about 17 months from 1854 to 2020. So, the good news is the U.S. economy is resilient, it always bounces back. But that still doesn't change the fact that a recession can wreak havoc in person's personal life. It still has the capacity to turn a person's life upside down!

It was interesting to find out that in my life time, since 1978 the year I was born according to Investopedia there has been six recessions! There was the Iran and Volcker Recession, part 1, from January 1980 to July 1980, then there was a part 2, a double dip in July of 1981 to November 1982. Then there was the Gulf war recession from July 1990 to March 1991. After that was the Dot-Com recession in March 2001 to November 2001. We can't forget about the Financial Crisis in December 2007 to June 2009, when the government bailed out all them banks. Then recently the Covid-19 recession from February 2020 to April 2020.

That's quite a few in my life time. Some of them I don't really remember. I was too young to understand, but the more recent ones I definitely learned a lot about the world I live in. I learned that there was such a thing as essential and non-essential workers. Something else I learned is recessions are inevitable. Get this, they are expected. They are believed to be on a 5-to-10-year cycle. Since that's the case it only makes sense that we prepare for them. Aside from the abuses of politicians, governments, yada-yada-yada what can you and I do to mitigate the impact of a recession? How can we live our life so that we go unscathed by a recession? Is it possible to weather the storm and not be affected? My answer, absolutely! There are six simple habits we can develop and teach our kids to empower them so that the fear & panic of a recession will be a thing of the past!

Chapter Two: Habit #1

Empower Yourself through Financial Literacy

I'm going to take a gamble here by being a little vulnerable. Hopefully what I share about myself won't cause you to disregard what I have to say, but instead get you to see the power of financial literacy. As a Hispanic born to teenage parents, who both dropped out of junior high school you can imagine the financial struggle we experienced just to make ends meet. Without going into too much detail I remember a lot of arguments over money. I used to love playing baseball. For me it was electric from the butterflies in my stomach when I took the field to hearing all the families cheering in the stands! I remember one particular year that money was so tight for my family my mother couldn't afford to pay the 60 dollars for my uniform. I didn't play that year. I was 10 years old at the time, I haven't played since.

So, growing up I had a general understanding of the importance of money but never understood the concept of money. I'm ashamed to say, because of this I made some bad choices chasing money as a juvenile. After getting in trouble with the law and realizing what I was doing goes against my new found faith I started to think maybe I'm going about this whole money thing wrong. No doubt money is important but maybe I've been ***hustling backwards*** this whole time. This insight set me on a course to learn about money. I started with checking out books in the library. First book I ever read that revolutionized my thinking about money was Rich Dad Poor Dad by Robert Kiyosaki. Even though he made his riches through real estate and at the time I wasn't in any position to purchase property there were some key concepts and ideas he talked about that has influenced how I think till this very day. For starters he believes if you don't start building your dream someone will **hire** you to build theirs! He also believes no one will ever become wealthy without first becoming a boss! This motivated me to be ambitious and want to become a boss.

    Next, I started to take some personal finance classes at the local college. I didn't set out to earn a degree only to get more knowledge. I felt I was definitely on the right track. At first, I was a little intimidated about going back to school especially because I never took school seriously and because of that failed to learn a lot of foundational things but I didn't let that keep me from what I was trying to achieve. I learned a lot of great things. But there was one thing that was talked about that really fascinated me but wasn't taught much about, stocks!

    I was back in the library and online, reading everything I could about stocks. I started out first reading children's books. One book in particular was Wow the Dow by Pat Smith. This book explained technical things in simple terms. Little did I know I was laying a foundation for myself in understanding the stock market and how it works. Through this process I not only was learning life changing concepts but I was learning the language of money. My financial knowledge was growing along with my confidence in learning this stuff.

    As my financial knowledge began to grow, I started to realize how uninformed my family and I were about money. I remember reading a quote that put my upbringing into perspective. The quote was: "Ignorance makes you vulnerable to be exploited". The way to empower myself and others was to become financially informed. I was discovering how a consistent habit of financial education will expose you to powerful life changing concepts that change how you view yourself and the world around you.

If you think about it people work hard to make money, but little effort is put into learning what to do with it when you make it. For many making money is not the problem. The problem is not knowing what to do with it when you make it. Auto Mechanics have a saying that can be applied here. They tell their young apprentice, "Work smarter not harder!" Our solution to every financial predicament we find ourselves in shouldn't be to get a second job. When that becomes our go to, we find ourselves living to work instead of working to live. Working two jobs, as noble as that may be, can only go on for so long before it leaves you depleted. Your days off are spent sleeping only to wake up and do it all again. Been there, done that, and don't want to go back to that!

Financial literacy on the other hand taught me how my money should work just as hard for me as I work for it. I learned about the pit falls of credit, I also learned the difference between good credit and bad credit. I learned how important budgeting and money management is to achieving your financial goals. If money doesn't have a destination than it will be spent on anything. I learned about building a six-month emergency fund for myself to prepare for unexpected events that occur in life, recession being one of them. I came to realize money isn't the end game, it's a means to an end. Money is the means we use to living the type and quality of life we desire for ourselves. I can go on and on, hopefully I've made my point.

The first step to **Recession Proofing Your Life is to develop a consistent habit of educating yourself about money**. Start by finishing this book. Then make it point to read one book a month, or listen to an audio book on your commute to work. Take a course online in the comforts of your home while you relax in your pjs. Whatever you decide to do remember consistency is how habits are formed!

Here's something you may not have known, during the financial crisis of 2007 the Amish community not only weathered the storm of that recession but were in a financial position to lend the government & businesses money they had saved (Money Secrets of the Amish: Finding True Abundance in Simplicity, Sharing, and Saving by Lorilee Craker). They are doing something right, techniques, practices I may need to incorporate into my own life!

Chapter Three: Habit #2

Always Invest in Yourself

One thing life has taught many of us is how nothing is certain. Life has changed so much from one generation to the next. Especially when it comes to business. My father worked for a company for 24 years of his life, when I say worked, I mean worked! He was there 5 in the morning. When they had hot jobs that needed to be finished, he was the first one to be asked to stay overtime. There were times he would work 14-hour shifts. He was committed to this company. He gave them his heart and soul. You probably can see where I'm going with this. The way they showed him their appreciation was to lay him off after 24 years of his life working for them. It's funny when I think back to how my father would pride himself about having no absences. At the time my father was laid off there was nothing funny about it. My parents had a mortgage payment. My father was the sole provider and had five mouths to feed. I'm sure you can imagine how devastating that time was for everyone.

My father's faith really sustained him during that time, but I learned something valuable in life through that whole experience. All my father was to that company was an expense. When the company decided to cut cost and make adjustments to their balance sheets and revenue his job was done away with. His family wasn't considered, his commitment to the company wasn't factored in the decision. At the end of the day, he was a number that was expendable, that's the nature of business. In the corporate offices decisions are made to cut whole departments because some board has decided to go in a different direction, that's the nature of business.

In 2017 Cisco Systems announced how they met analyst expectations, expected earning of $.60 a share. In fact, they made $.63 cents a share which implies business was good. The board and executives of the company decided to axe their manufacturing department and focus their attention on data storing "clouding." What that meant was 45,000 jobs that make up their manufacturing department would be gone. Keep in mind they weren't fired for performance reasons simply someone decided that the company was going to go in a new direction, the nature of business.

Now let's consider how technology is changing the landscape of the economy. Whole industries have been and are being replaced by technology. Companies are realizing it's cheaper to purchase software than keep whole departments. The more technology advances the more jobs are in jeopardy. A few years ago, I read an article where two tech-employment scholars by the names Carl Frey and Michael Osborne predicted within two decades forty-seven percent of all U.S. jobs will be automated.

What this means is all the career planning in the world cannot prepare a person for the nature of business. It's heartless and cutthroat. Even with having a career you have to prepare for unforeseeable events. Unforeseeable events are basically you finding yourself saying "I didn't see that coming…" Some unforeseeable events can be:

- Company moves out of state or country
- Replaced by technology
- Service you provide is replaced by software or outsourced to someone cheaper
- Merger & acquisition decides to lay everyone off and start fresh
- You pick a field that is no longer adding jobs.

The take away in all this is we're all expendable. No matter who you are. Think of the most recent example, Covid-19. Unexpectedly, a lot of businesses were either in jeopardy of closing their doors indefinitely or did. The sooner we understand this the better we're off. No surprises, no excuses. All that is left is for us to be proactive.

Whenever you find yourself in a 9 to 5 you cannot afford to get complacent. There is no such thing as job security. Instead, you must learn to change and adapt to the times. You do that by making yourself valuable through investing in yourself! Long gone are the days when you could work for a company, grow with the company, and make a livable wage with that company.

What are some ways you can invest in yourself? It's a proven fact that companies hire internally to fill positions before they go outside the company. Take a class in preparation for that potential position opening up. Being proactive is expanding your knowledge and skill set by learning different things related to your field. If you're in sales that can mean taking a class in human resources. Look for opportunities of mobility within your company. When you're working for a company, you learn a lot of things through the grapevine. You learn about who is retiring, who is moving, or transferring to a different department. Start positioning yourself.

But also think about opportunities in other areas. Do your research. Find out what industries and jobs in those industries are growing and start taking classes. What's a growing field. Also, consider how you're changing. I got into construction because I love to build. Then, I became a certified wielder. As I'm getting older, I'm thinking more and more about the type of work I want to do. Since I have a passion to help others and struggled in my youth with addiction, I decided to become a certified Substance Abuse Counselor. Don't put any limit on yourself! Maybe it's time to chase your passion.

The next step to **Recession Proofing Your Life is to invest in your yourself**. The greatest asset you have that doesn't fluctuate with the market and always pays dividends is **Yourself!** Making yourself valuable creates options and opportunities.

Chapter Four: Habit #3

Value Your Time

While we were on vacation my son turned two. There was a moment when I just stared at him and thought about how much has happened in the last two years. From one moment to the next he was walking. And out nowhere, without any prompting in the morning when he gets up and realizes I'm not in bed he starts yelling, "Dad, dad?" These are all precious moments I thank God I was present for.

Then there's my parents. I moved two hours away from them, so I don't get a chance to visit them often. But we make it a point to get together in order to strengthen our relationship. Every time we come together, I see how my parents are getting much older and they can't do the same things they used to. More and more I can see how they are needing assistance with basic daily things. That wasn't always the case. I grew up with both my parents working hard and spending long hours at work because they wanted to buy our family a house that we can call our own. But, in the process they missed out on a lot of my childhood milestones. Chasing the American dream cost more than money it cost the most valuable thing we all have, *Time*!

We often hear people talk about how they would like to provide for their family a better life than they had growing up which is common and natural for people to think and feel but the problem is there isn't much difference in the *quality of life* they are envisioning. Quality isn't found in the material things you have. You can have a big house but no one's ever home to enjoy it. You can give your children the best & latest toys on the market but they're still left alone to figure those toys out, you can fill their days with activities but they have no one on the sideline cheering for them, that's basically how I grew up!

As I mentioned earlier my parents had me as teenagers, initially it was tough making ends meet. Some of the stories my mother shared with me I was too young to remember but nonetheless heart breaking to imagine. But fortunately, they got into a growing field and worked their way up despite their lack of education. They found themselves relying heavily on their experience. This allowed them to become experts in their field. Now their resume is filled with companies like McDonald Douglas, Boeing, Teledyne, Northrop, etc. But all of it at a cost. Sure, we moved from a studio apartment to a larger house. But, for years I remember tucking myself into bed. Sure, we had stuff, but I still found myself in places where I felt seen. None of that stuff filled the absence of my parents I felt inside. You can have a whole family living under one roof but still feel alone. As odd as this may sound it wasn't until my 30's did I come to learn what my parents did for a living. When I started to work on myself it was in that process I realized how disconnected I was and how there was so much I didn't know about my family.

This *devaluation of time* is very subtle. Oftentimes you don't realize it is happening until it is too late. My wife was vital in me coming to learn this lesson. I'm no different, I too told myself I'm going to provide a better life for my family than I had growing up. I can't say I knew exactly what that meant, but I did know I wanted to be present for my family in a way that I didn't get to experience my parents' presence growing up. I live in Upland, California. Upland is in the San Bernadino County area which is a two-hour drive from Los Angeles. I was offered a really great job in Los Angeles that was going to pay really well. I was excited to share the news with my wife who then put it all into perspective for me. She was really happy for me to have the opportunity to build my resume. She started to calculate the commute and most likely the overtime I'll be doing and came up with 12-to-14-hour days. What she said next was really what hit me the hardest, she said, "The money is really not that great when you consider how much you are going to miss out on your son's life!" She was totally right, by the time I got home he'll be either going to bed or asleep only to have me do it all over again the next day.

  American culture teaches us status symbols is what life is all about. These status symbols are everything from name brand shoes, clothes, to what a person drives, and where a person lives. They give the illusion as if we have arrived or that we are somehow living the American dream because of them but they fail to mention how we lose ourselves in the pursuit of them. It's amazing to see how inflation is at ten percent yet the malls are more packed than ever! We don't realize how status symbols can serve as identity markers. But in the end, it only produces shallow, indifferent people. People of character with depth of person only comes by way of investing time and being present. When a person is present to seize and take advantage of those teachable moments' intimacy is created, solidified and character is built.

The next step to **Recession Proofing Your Life is to Value Your Time**. When I learned to value my time, I had to replace instant gratification for delayed gratification. I went from being near sighted to thinking long term. I went from being materialistic to being simplistic. I went from discontent to being content. When you value your time, you're not so quick to give it away because you understand you won't get any of it back. You and only you are responsible for how you spend your time! The time you have should be spent on building, investing, and nurturing the life and family you want to be and enjoy!

Proverbs 17:1 says, "Better is a dry morsel with quiet than a house full of feasting with strife."

Steve Jobs' fact of life before he died said,"1. Don't educate your children to be rich. Educate them to be happy. So, when they grow up, they will know the *value of things* not the price."

Chapter Five: Habit #4

Life Management

When you start to value time, you search for ways to get more of it! When you begin to value time, you naturally look for ways to get the most out of the time you have. This is where time management comes in. But the thing about time management is no one can manage time. Time can be a friend or foe, it's ruthless in the sense once it's lost there's no getting it back. Time continues whether you want it to or not. Since we can't manage time, the one thing we can manage to get the most out of time is our lives. **Life management** is the only way to manage time in order to make the most of the time we have.

First, I have to admit on a daily basis I have more things to do than I have time to do them! When you think about time how many actual hours a day do we have to work with? I'm not a math wiz but I'm going to give this a shot. There's 24 hours in a day. Eight of those hours are devoted to sleeping and getting ready for work. Then another 9 hours is devoted to work and the commute to work. Already, 17 hours gone! Which leaves me with 7 hours. Wait, I forgot to mention a couple of hours scrolling my phone and keeping up with social media. I make it a point to eat dinner with my wife and son there's another hour gone. Then my son and I usually spend an hour in the backyard playing on his slide and riding his bike. That leaves me with three hours, but I can't forget to mention talking with my wife about the day and other things we need to do. Also, I'll spend 15 minutes here, 15 minutes there answering phone calls and talking with family & friends. Well, it turns out I have no time left during the week, maybe I'll wait for my days off...

It's no wonder why I find myself frustrated, feeling like I'm not getting anything done or getting ahead. Life can feel as if I'm at a standstill. This is why life management is so important. In order to develop habit #1 (Financial Literacy) & habit #2 (Investing in Yourself) you need *time* for those things. In order to get ahead time management is a necessity, better said **Life management**.

What does life management look like? What does that even mean. Life management is investing and maintaining the things that are important to you without losing yourself in the process. Of course, this can mean different things to different people. But, the purpose of it is to make the most and get the most out of the time you have. How exactly do you do that, first start with a time journal. It's human nature to develop routines for ourselves without even realizing it. Spend a couple weeks writing down your daily routine, how you are spending your time. Leave nothing out! A thirty-minute conversation here, scrolling on my phone for 45 minutes. Surfing the web. Whatever you do. Account for every hour of the day. That's usually a good place to begin with because you can easily pin point areas that need to be managed a little better and areas you need to spend a little more time in. You would be surprise at what you learn.

It's easy to busy yourself with doing things but the key to making the most of your time is to busy yourself with productive, life advancing things. Once you have an idea of how you're spending your time you can readjust your routine in order to get the most out of the hours you have to work with. Instead of wasting hours scrolling and surfing the net you spend that time taking an online course. There are two disciplines that go hand in hand with life management. They are organizational skills and scheduling. Both organizational skills and scheduling are necessary to not only meet certain obligations but also to manage all the various things going on in life. Organizational skills is believed to not only reduce a person's stress level, but also increases a person's productivity. I read somewhere 90 percent of success can be attributed to being organized, from corporations to a person's personal life. Life management is learning to be more organized.

Scheduling on the other hand takes skill. It's the art of planning your activities. When done well you can achieve goals and priorities in the time you have available. Scheduling is the process you use to plan how you'll spend your time. So much can be done by developing both these disciplines. It takes time and consistency to become effective at them both.

The necessity of both these disciplines really came into focus for me when I went back to school. In order to meet deadlines, and still make time for my family and myself I had to sit down at the dinner table with a monthly calendar on one side of me and a list of things to do on the other side. It was the consistent commitment to the schedule I designed for myself that allowed me to achieve the goals of finishing my degrees, opening my own business, and still having time for myself – something we'll talk more about in the next chapter.

Every Sunday my wife and I get together and fill out a template we pulled from the internet called Weekly Spouse Meeting Agenda. It covers the following areas:

1. Finances
2. Appointments/Weekend Plans
3. Goals/Projects Check In
4. Questions & Concerns
5. Gratitude

We've managed to get so much done by sticking with this weekly practice. There are times we get busy and forget to do it, not a problem. We simply get back to the routine of doing it again.

Another step to *Recession Proofing Your Life is Life Management*. Time is relentless, it stops for no one! The only way for us to get the most out of the time we have is by developing the discipline of being organized and mastering the art of scheduling. Both are essential for *Life Management*!

Chapter Six: Habit #5

Self-Care

Self-Care is a rather new term to an age-old practice. The spirit of it has existed since the beginning of time. Clinicians come up with these nifty terms to describe things that have gone on for years. So, what is Self-Care? A quick Google search you'll come up with things like:

> "The practice of taking an active role in protecting one's own well-being and happiness, in particular during periods of stress."

> "Self-care is important to maintaining a healthy relationship with yourself. It means doing things to take care of our minds, bodies, and souls by engaging in activities that promote well-being and reduce stress. Doing so enhances our ability to live fully, vibrantly, and effectively. The practice of self-care also reminds both you and others that your needs are valid and a priority."

In my line of work Self-Care is one of the most neglected areas in a person's life. By the time they arrive they have lost all connection with themselves. No one is exempt from that happening. It's really easy to lose that connection with yourself simply by just working and living life. You can't imagine how many times I've asked a person to tell me about themselves, and they're at a loss of words. They often respond with I don't know? What are your favorite hobbies? What do you do for fun? How do you spend your leisure time? Where do you go for peace of mind? These are questions we should have answers to.

  I can't overstate the benefits of developing a habit of good, healthy Self-Care. Have you ever experienced burnout? I've read cases where a person literally worked themselves into a nervous breakdown. The body begins to shut itself down. This is why it is extremely important to get acquainted with yourself. Know when you may need to sleep in on the weekend or know when you need a power nap throughout the day. Know when your frustration level is shrinking and you find yourself a little edgy, these are all indicators it's time for some "Me time." Self-Care would include spirituality. When you are taking adequate care of yourself which means you're eating well, sleeping and resting enough, pursuing your hobbies, spending time in your quiet place you will see how your performance level is so much better than when these areas are being neglected.

  I'm sure we've all come across that person who is overworked or maybe been that person think about how much suffers because that person has failed to take some time for him or herself to rejuvenate, and refresh. In substance use treatment one of the things that is taught as potential triggers is the acronym H.A.L.T. which stands for hunger, anger, lonely, tired. It requires some self-awareness to be able to identify when these areas need attention from us. These are basic human needs that need to be taken care of. When we find ourselves neglecting them it shows in our performance and unfortunately in our relationship with those closes to us.

  One of my close friends, Chris was really good at pointing this out to me. He would always tell me, "Rey, you're burning the candle from both ends! It's time to smell the roses." I knew exactly what he meant. I'm one of those persons that will keep going, and going. I try to pack as much as I can in a day all the while I'm telling myself I'm almost done only to go to the next project once I'm finished with the one I'm working on. I need those constant reminders to stop and smell the roses.

It's easy to convince yourself why you need to keep going and put off that time for yourself, but when you consider the benefits and dangers of Self-Care you can't afford to neglect the one thing that is keeping the whole ship moving forward, You! This habit is just as important as the other habits mentioned and even more so, because if your health starts to give way because of neglect or relationships began to suffer all this work and effort becomes pointless.

Remember Self-Care is just as important as all the other habits mentioned so far! As you are developing and maintaining the habits of *empowering yourself through financial literacy*, *investing in yourself*, *valuing your time*, and *life management* be sure to create balance for yourself through Self-Care. When you think about it, serenity is priceless! To find a hobby, a passion or a place where you lose all track of time, how can one put a price on that? We deserve to live our best life, but it's entirely up to us to create the balance needed to experience that best life!

My parents are a great example how it's never too late to find that place of serenity. My mother at sixty spends her days at a nearby park feeding the squirrels and talking with other people who frequent the park, about life. She tells me how peaceful it is for her and how rejuvenated she feels after spending the afternoon there. My father on the other hand finds his serenity relaxing in his lazy-boy chair, eating his favorite snacks while watching a good movie! Both remind me and leave me thinking about my place of serenity?

The fifth habit to **Recession Proofing Your Life is maintaining good, healthy Self-Care**. As the sole provider for my family, I always consider the things I get myself involved in. I can't afford an injury that will keep me from fulfilling this duty. The same can be applied to the purpose of this book. If you're not taking adequate care of yourself, how do you hope to not only live your best life but also maintain a quality of life for you and your family? What are you doing to smell the Roses?

Chapter Seven: Habit #6

Try New Things

It's amazing how simply being creatures of habit will keep us from venturing out and experiencing new things, robbing us of so much the world has to offer and what we can give. Some of the major growth spurts in my personal development came from me forcing myself out of my comfort zone.

You might be asking, "What does trying new things have to do with recession proofing my life?" For me, trying new things is not only necessary for personal growth, but by developing a habit of trying new things you never know what you may discover about yourself. You may just stumble into a new found passion. That newly discovered passion may turn around and become the new career that replaces your boring monotonous, underpaid job you currently have.

Serendipitous: /ˌserənˈdipədəs/
adjective
1. occurring or discovered by chance in a happy or beneficial way.

Serendipity: /ˌserənˈdipədē/
Noun
2. an unplanned fortunate discovery.

When I learned what the word serendipitous (serendipity) meant I fell in love with the word because it's pretty much how life works. From new inventions, to personal discoveries. If I were to reflect on my life what I've experienced, what I'm doing today from writing this book to starting a non-profit I can go on and on and on it can all be traced back to **being open to trying new things**! Growing up I had an extremely hard time with public speaking. I didn't realize it was a problem until I tried to do it. I remember the very first time I tried to speak in a group setting I began to hyperventilate; I was gasping for air so much that I couldn't complete an entire sentence. This was a nuisance for me because I felt like I had something to say and my opinion was just as valid as the next person. I took a toastmaster's class at the recommendation of a friend and slowly but surely began to overcome this public speaking phobia. Little did I know this would prepare me for a career in public speaking from teaching workshops, to holding seminars.

A couple years ago a good friend of mine, Daniel, was telling me about his new business venture and how it was pretty successful. He was able to get his farm certified with the city which allowed him to start selling organic produce at local Farmer's Market. Now he's his own boss, he has 11 markets that he sells at and a handful of employees. He grew up in the city. He never thought he'd be a farmer and a successful one at that!

There are so many examples we can draw on that shows just how important developing a habit of trying new things is. What I've come to realize in my own personal life is the more I try new things the more confidence I have to take on new projects. I didn't always have this openness to try new things. Before I came to the place where I am today which is a growth mindset my first thought or reaction to trying new things was, I can't do that! I don't want to make a fool of myself, or I don't know how to do that! It was always a limiting belief, a belief that kept me away from the opportunity to grow. It's what is called a fixed mindset. At the time I didn't realize I had a fixed mindset. A *fixed mindset* believes basic qualities like intelligence or talent, are simply fixed traits. So, what you have is all you got! Whereas a growth mindset is the opposite. A *growth mindset* believes basic abilities can be developed through dedication and hard work.

In order for me to go from having a fixed mindset to a growth mindset I had to set aside my limiting beliefs and simply be open to trying new things. And in time it gave me the confidence and motivation to be willing to take on anything. Now my thoughts and reactions are let's do this, when do we start?! Having a growth mindset can also contribute to the quality of life you desire to have. You're able to inspire and motivate others do as you have done, try new things!

You're probably thinking trying new things, where do I start? It can be something as simple as volunteering. Everyone has a comfort zone they rather live and thrive in. Look for ways to step out of that zone. You'll come to learn the more you do that the more your comfort zone will expand. So much good can come out of trying new things, things like new friendships, new contacts, new opportunities, new passions, new perspectives, new directions, and a whole new life experience!

The sixth final habit to *Recession Proofing Your Life is trying new things*. Life is too short to be stuck in routines, patterns, or living life imprisoned to limiting beliefs! Living your best life while maintaining your quality of life can mean different things for different people but the one thing we all have in common is the desire for stability. If it wasn't you wouldn't be reading this book. Stability means adapting to changing times. Adapting may come through trying new things.

Chapter Eight: Conclusion

Consistency

I read somewhere it takes 21 days of consistent practice to form a habit. It turns out the latest research has discredited that and now claims it takes an average of 66 days, typical. Whatever the case may be to form a habit it requires **consistent practice**! Whether 21 or 66, it requires you doing it when you don't feel like it! In order to make these six habits second nature to who you are it's going to require you to be consistent. Those who have achieved much in life can tell you all about being consistent. Consistency is a dying attribute, its underutilized and undervalued. But when you consider it, consistency has enabled people to do phenomenal things. It can help you achieve any goal you set for yourself all it requires is for you to establish the time and place. What Consistency is, consistency is you showing up, day in and day out!

Here's an acronym that will help you to remember these 6 habits, Finaly! I've found acronyms to be very helpful in memorizing important things. Don't get hung up on the misspelling, you have to find a way to make it work!

F – Financial Literacy

I – Invest in Yourself

N – Never allow others to determine the value of your time.

A – Always make the most of your time through life management.

L – Love thy self through self-care.

Y – Yearn for new things.

Life is happening and it will continue to happen whether you show up or not! Living these six habits will make sure you show up!

Acknowledgments

I would like to thank my wife who supports and assists me in all the different endeavors I hope to accomplish in life. I would like to thank my family who believed in me and were there for me during my darkest hour. I would also like to thank my friends for the feedback they gave me about this important topic. Last, but definitely not least I would like to thank God for the new lease on life He's given me and the perspective to appreciate it and make the most with what He's given me!

About the Author

Reynaldo Aguilar is a lover of knowledge. He is self-taught and knowledgeable in many areas. He holds a paralegal degree, has an associate in Business and Behavioral & Social Science. He has a certification as an Addiction Drug Specialist 1 & 2. He is a certified Substance Use Counselor.

Reynaldo Aguilar is founder and President of RTime Co., a non-profit company which teaches workshops from Financial Literacy to Substance Abuse Relapse Prevention.

Reynaldo Aguilar is currently facilitating rehabilitative workshops in the California prison system. He collaborates with other organizations to achieve the goal of healing and restoration.

www.ingramcontent.com/pod-product-compliance
Lightning Source LLC
Chambersburg PA
CBHW050306220526
45465CB00002B/850